Spelling Made Easy

Level 1

Teacher's Textbook
(Revised)

Key Stages 1 & 2

Age Group 5-8 Years

Best selling Multi-Sensory Structured Phonics

by Violet Brand

Introduction

Violet Brand's highly successful 'Spelling Made Easy' series originated in her diagnostic work with young adults with reading difficulties between 1975 and 1980. Multi-sensory phonic-based reading and spelling methods were unfashionable at the time so she created her own teaching material. This was published in 1984 and became widely used, in particular for one-to-one tuition.

Violet always maintained that if a pupil could spell they could read.

The Revised 'Spelling Made Easy' Text Books (publ 2012) are faithful to the original structure and sequence but the range has been updated to include:

- Expanded initial word lists to encompass early introduction of the synthetic phonics sequence
- Synthetic phonics sequence highlighted in Red Introductory Book
- Additional material included in Red Introductory Level and Green Level 1 books
- New 'pupil friendly' typeface
- Texts modernised and updated as required with completely new text for Purple Book Level 3

The highly important original features of the series are still present including:

- The clearly defined incremental sequence of sounds including phonemes and blends
- Word lists for each sound to be taught word by word in a 'listen, say and write' sequence. Violet Brand's original suggested teaching method, using the 'a' sound for instance, was:

  (a) Write the sound in red on a board – saying it

  (b) Show card with the family of words written in 'blackboard' size

  (c) Cover all words but 'cat' – children read it

  (d) Gradually uncover all words until full list is seen and read

  (e) Draw attention of children to common sound/symbol in all of the words

  (f) Pupils write the words as teacher dictates them

  (g) Encourage all pupils to quietly say the sounds as they write them

- A dictation accompanies each new word list for pupils to write out and then identify words with the featured sounds
- 'High frequency' words are introduced early
- 'Teaching points' focus on possible areas of difficulty with practical suggestions to work on these.

BrandBooks 2012

Contents

Sound	Page	Sound	Page	Sound	Page
a	1	ai	18	y (ī)	35
o	2	oa	19	ow (ō)	36
i	3	ir	20	ew	37
e	4	ou(ow)	21	tion	38
u	5	ea (ĕ)	22	oy	39
ck	6	ay	23	au	40
ee	7	ing	24	ī	41
oo and oo(u)	8	ur	25	ear	42
ar	9	aw	26	air	43
or	10	oi	27	ou(ŭ)	44
sh	11	er	28	a (ŏ)	45
ch	12	all - al	29	ph	46
th	13	ea (ĕ)	30	o (ō)	47
a_e	14	ow	31	are (air)	48
i_e	15	igh	32	ough	49
o_e	16	a (ar)	33	ar (or)	50
u_e	17	o (ŭ)	34		

Additional and ancillary material for the sounds listed above is available in Spelling Made Easy 'Fun with Phonics' Level 1 Worksheets (Page references in brackets)

a,o,e,i,u — Fun with Phonics pp 2-5
ck,ee,oo,ar,or — Fun with Phonics pp 6-9
sh,ch,th,a-e,i-e — Fun with Phonics pp10-13
o-e,u-e,ai,oa,ir — Fun with Phonics pp14-17
ou,ea,ay,ing,ur — Fun with Phonics pp18-21
aw,oi,all,er,ea — Fun with Phonics pp 22-25
ow,igh,a,o,y — Fun with Phonics pp26-29
ow,ew,tion,au,i,oy — Fun with Phonics pp30-33
ear,ai,ou,a,ph — Fun with Phonics pp34-37
o,are,ough,ar — Fun with Phonics pp38-41

Spelling Made Easy Level 1 A4 Text Book (Revised)
by Violet Brand
First published in the United Kingdom in 2012

© Copyright assigned to BrandBooks (a division of G & M Brand Publications Ltd) and Violet Brand who asserts her moral rights as the author.

ISBN 978-1-904421-21-4 All rights reserved. www.spellingmadeeasy.co.uk

The copyright of all materials in the 'Spelling Made Easy' series remains the property of the publisher and the author. No part of this book may be reproduced or translated in any form or by any means, electronic or mechanical, including recording or by an information storage or retrieval system without permission in writing from the publisher.

"The multi-sensory methods of teaching spelling seem to have been overlooked in recent main-stream education. Too much emphasis has been placed on learning to spell through visual methods. The ears and the mouth have been forgotten and the power of the hand ignored.

If a child, or an adult, hears a sequence of sounds, sees them visually represented, feels the sequence in their mouth and reproduces the symbols with their hand, their awareness of the basis of written language is awakened. They feel that they can control it - and what they control they can use. No one sense is left to flounder and the fear of the printed word which so often besets adult illiterates and failing teenagers is removed"

(Violet Brand MBE Introduction to 1984 editions)

a

h **a** n d	c r **a** m p
s **a** n d	t r **a** m p
s p **a** t	s p r **a** n g
b **a** n g	s c r **a** p s
b **a** n k	

Dictate the Sam and the Tramp Story

The tramp had cramp as he sat with his scraps on the bank. A rat sprang from the sand. The tramp spat at the rat and ran.

Pupils draw a line under the words in the 'a' family.

New words: the, he, with, his, on, from

Read the Grandad Bill Story

Bang! Clang! Grandad Bill sat in Sad Gran's van. It spat and sprang off. Grandad Bill had to go to the bank. He had damp sand in the back of the van and Sad Gran's cat ran from the sand and sat on his hand.

Grandad gave it a slap with his cap. Bang! The bad cat ran, but Sad Gran's van ran up a plank on a ramp and back onto Sad Gran's land.

Pupils identify and write 2 words ending in 'amp' and 2 words ending in 'and'.

Teaching Points
(a) Help children to feel '**n**' in hand, sand, bang, bank and sprang. Help them to feel '**m**' in cramp, tramp.
(b) Help children feel 'sp', 'cr', 'tr', 'spr', 'scr' and 'ps'.
(c) Discuss capital letters at beginning of sentences and full stops at the end.

o

dr**o**p	pl**o**t
sp**o**t	cr**o**ss
c**o**st	g**o**ng
p**o**nd	sl**o**t
fr**o**st	str**o**ng
l**o**st	

Dictate the Sam and the Tramp Story

The cross tramp ran to a spot by the pond. He had lost his scraps, but he had a plot to trap the rat.

Pupils draw a line under the words in the 'o' family.

New words: to, by, but

Read the Grandad Bill Story

Sad Gran was cross. "Stop. Stop," she said. She was cross with Grandad Bill.

Grandad was hot and began to flap his cap.

Grandad got a long rod from the van. He had the long rod in his hand and gave the van a prod.

"Stop. Grandad Bill," said Sad Gran. "Drop that rod."

Pupils identify and write 2 words ending in 'od'.

Teaching Points
(a) Feel 'n' in pond, gong, strong.
(b) Feel 's' in cost, frost, lost.
(c) Feel 'dr', 'sp', 'fr', 'pl', 'cr', 'sl', 'str'.
(d) Draw attention to 'ss' on cross.
(e) Discuss use of comma.

i

r **i** n g   d r **i** n k
k **i** n g   s t r **i** n g
s t **i** n g   c r **i** s p s
m **i** n t   p **i** c n **i** c
t r **i** p

Dictate the Sam and the Tramp Story

    The tramp had a string bag. He had crisps in the bag. He sat by the pond and had a drink. The rat ran into the string bag.

Pupils draw a line under the words in the 'i' family.

New word: into

Read the Grandad Bill Story

    Clang, clink. The van began to tip and slip off the ramp.
    "The plank on the ramp will split," said Sad Gran.
    The plank did split and Sad Gran's van began to sink into the soft sand. Sad Gran began to hiss.
    "Grip the van and lift it off the split plank," she said.
    Grandad bit his lip and began to lift.

Pupils identify and write 4 words ending in 'ip'.

Teaching Points
(a) Feel consonant blends, especially 'str' and 'sps'.
(b) Discuss pic/nic.

e

d **e** s k	f **e** l l
t **e** n t	s m **e** l l
s **e** n t	y **e** l l
f **e** l t	d r **e** s s
h **e** l d	l **e** f t

Dictate the Sam and the Tramp Story

The tramp felt the rat in the bag and held it in his strong hand. He let it smell the crisps. Then, he fell and sent the rat into the pond. He kept the bag in his hand.

Pupils draw a line under the words in the 'e' family.

New word: then

Read the Grandad Bill Story

Grandad Bill held the van.
"Help. Help," yelled Grandad Bill as he felt the van slip.
The West twins ran from Sad Gran's to help as well.
Grandad felt strong and said, "Get set, lift."
Grandad Bill, Sad Gran and the West twins held the van.
Grandad got a plank and set it on the ramp.
"Get set," he said. "Let the van drop."

Pupils identify and write 3 words using 'el' or 'ell'.

Teaching Points

(a) Draw attention to words ending in 'll' and 'ss'.
(b) Feel consonant blends, particularly 'lt', 'ld' and 'ft'.

u

d r **u** m	b **u** n k
d **u** s t	p l **u** g
j **u** s t	s c r **u** b
l **u** m p	h **u** n d r e d
b **u** m p	s **u** n s e t

Dictate the Sam and the Tramp Story

The tramp had a lump on his leg from the bump. He had no rat in his bag, just dust. The sun set and he held the lump on his leg as he slept. He had no bed and no bunk.

Pupils draw a line under the words in the 'u' family.

New word: no

Read the Grandad Bill Story

Sad Gran, Grandad Bill and the West twins let the van drop. The twins fell with a yell in the dust and Grandad had a lump on his left hand.

Grandad gave a gulp. Sad Gran's van had a big bump in it.

"I must get to the bank," he said. "This big bump in the van will cost a lot."

"Hundreds, Grandad Bill," said Sad Gran.

Pupils identify and write 2 words ending in 'ump'.

Teaching Points

(a) Draw attention to 'e' in hundred.
(b) Discuss the difference between 'The sunset' and 'The sun set'.

ck

clo**ck**	tri**ck**
bri**ck**	tra**ck**
du**ck**	pe**ck**
lu**ck**	pri**ck**
sna**ck**	stru**ck**
qui**ck**	

Dictate the Sam and the Tramp Story

The tramp had bad luck. As he slept, a duck had a peck at his legs and the rat ran back for a quick snack of crisps. The clock struck ten and the tramp sat up.

Sam is at the pond.

Pupils draw a line under the words in the 'ck' family.

Read the Grandad Bill Story

Grandad got back into Sad Gran's van.
"Bad luck Grandad Bill," said the West Twins.
A clock struck twelve.
"Quick, Grandad," said Sad Gran. "Get to the bank."
"Can we sit on the sand in the back of the van and go with you to the bank?" said the twins.
"Get in quick," said Grandad and backed the van off Sad Gran's land and along the track.

Pupils identify and write 4 words ending in 'ck'.

Teaching Points
(a) As 'ck' together always follow a short vowel, this family can be used to revise short vowel sounds.
(b) Talk about five vowel sounds. Listen hard for which one it is.
(c) Point out that 'u' always follows 'q' in the English language.

ee

str**ee**t	scr**ee**n
w**ee**k	h**ee**l
qu**ee**n	n**ee**d
sp**ee**d	s**ee**d
st**ee**p	sw**ee**p
b**ee**	gr**ee**d

Dictate the Sam and the Tramp Story

The Queen is in the street and Sam needs to sweep the steep track to the pond. The tramp stands up. In his speed, his heel hits a bee. It stings.

Pupils draw a line under the words in the 'ee' family.

Read the Grandad Bill Story

Grandad Bill went at speed to the bank. The West twins held on in the back, as the van went up a steep street.

At the bank, Grandad said to the twins, "Keep still. I will go into the bank and then we will get a quick snack."

Grandad went into the bank and a big bee fell onto the damp sand in the van.

"Quick! Sweep the bee and the sand into the street," said Holly West as the bee struck her feet.

Pupils identify and write 2 words ending in 'eet' and 1 word ending in 'eed'.

Teaching Points
(a) Remind that 'u' follows q.
(b) Discuss capital letters for names – Queen.
(c) Discuss – (i) week – meaning days of the week.
        (ii) seeds – for the garden.
        (iii) heel – of the foot.
        (iv) bee – insect.
        (v) screen – television and cinema.
(d) Discuss 'y' making **ee** sound at the end of greedy.

oo and oo (ŭ)

Dictate the Sam and the Tramp Story

Sam held his broom and had a look at the tramp. The tramp took his boot off to look at his heel. The Queen is on the steep track to the pool and the tramp has no boot on his foot.

Pupils draw a line under the words in the 'oo' and 'oo' (ŭ) family.

New word: off

Read the Grandad Bill Story

Harry West took a broom and began to sweep sand and the big bee into the street.

Zoom, zoom went the bee and hit the roof of the van. Zoom, zoom went the bee and hit the heel of Holly's boot.

"Look," yelled Holly. "Quick. The big bee will get me."

Harry West took the broom to get the bee from Holly's boot.

"Stop," said Grandad Bill as he got back from the bank. "You will hit Holly."

Zoom, zoom. The bee went back to the street to look for food. Grandad Bill and the twins went to look for food too.

Pupils identify and write 2 words ending in 'oom' and 1 word ending in 'ood'.

Teaching Points
(a) In some areas a change of sound will occur between 'zoom' and 'look'. Discuss this.
(b) Discuss bed/room.

ar

c **ar**
c **a r** d
y **a r** d
  a r m
f **a r** m

g **a r** d e n
h **a r** d
m **a r** k
s m **a r** t
t **a r**

Dictate the Sam and the Tramp Story

The Queen looks hard at the tramp. He is not smart and his foot is as black as tar. She lifts her arm and Sam lifts his broom. The tramp just looks at the bee on his foot.

Pupils draw a line under the words in the 'ar' family.

New word: she

Read the Grandad Bill Story

Grandad Bill took the twins to a coffee bar. They left the van in the car park.

At the coffee bar, they sat on smart stools for fizzy drinks, crisps and jam tart. The jam tart was hard and Grandad Bill said, "A bad mark for the coffee bar. This jam tart is too hard."

They cut back across a yard to the car park.

"Oh no!" said Grandad Bill.

"Oh no!" said Harry West.

"Oh yes!" said Holly West. "The tar in the yard is wet. We are stuck."

Pupils identify and write 2 words ending in 'ard' and 2 words ending in 'art'.

Teaching Points

(a) Draw attention to non-sounding 'e' in 'garden'
(b) Discuss – (i) 'yard' – back-yard, builder's yard, etc.
          (ii) 'mark' and 'marks'.
          (iii) 'smart' (appearance) and 'smart' (clever).
          (iv) tar – the smell, the look, the use.

or

o r	f o r t y
b o r n	s t o r y
t o r n	f o r g e t
f o r	m o r n i n g
f o r t	m o r e

Dictate the Sam and the Tramp Story

The tramp will not forget the morning he met the Queen. The forty TV men will tell the sad story on the screen, but Sam thinks of the torn boots of the tramp. "We must get more boots and a hot drink," he says.

Pupils draw a line under the words in the 'or' family?

New words: TV, says

Read the Grandad Bill Story

"I forgot the wet tar in the yard," said Grandad Bill. "Stand still."

The man from the coffee bar stood at the end of the yard and looked hard at Grandad and the twins. "You are having a bad morning, Grandad," he said. "I can see a big bump in the van too."

"I forgot the wet tar," said Grandad.

"We will free you in forty seconds," said the man. He got a plank from the back of the coffee bar.

"Boots off," said the man from the coffee bar. "Forget the boots and get onto the plank in your socks."

Grandad Bill and the twins left the boots stuck in the tar and in a second more, they stood on the hard plank.

Pupils identify and write 3 words in the 'or' family.

Teaching Points

(a) Remind 'y' making 'ee' sound on forty and story.
(b) Draw attention to 'e' on more.
(c) Discuss for/get.
(d) Feel i-n-g on 'morning'.
(e) Show picture of fort.
(f) Discuss for – 'for me', 'for tea', etc.
(g) Speech marks.

sh

sh e d	c a **sh**
sh e e t	c r a **sh**
sh i p	r u **sh**
sh o t	s p l a **sh**

Dictate the Sam and the Tramp Story

Sam took the tramp to his shed.
"I will rush to get a hot drink for us," he said.
The tramp sat on a sheet of wood and went back to sleep.
Crash! Sam shot into the shed.
"I forgot my cash," he said.

Pupils draw a line under the words in the 'sh' family.

New words: said, my

Read the Grandad Bill Story

"Do not rush," said Grandad Bill. "We will creep along the plank." Grandad Bill and the West twins crept along the short plank and stood at the end of the yard.

"I wish we had boots on," said Holly West.

"Shut up," said Harry West. "Forget the boots."

"Sad Gran will be cross," said Holly.

"We will rush to the shop with my cash from the bank and get you more boots," said Grandad.

"Don't forget the bump in the van," said the man from the coffee bar. "You will have no cash left, Grandad."

Pupils identify and write 3 words ending in 'sh'.

Teaching Points

(a) Remind about use of speech marks and discuss.

ch

cheek	lun**ch**
chop	ben**ch**
chicken	crun**ch**
chip	su**ch**
chest	

Dictate the Sam and the Tramp Story

The tramp and Sam sat on the bench. The tramp had fish for his lunch and Sam had a chicken. They had lots of chips.

"I feel good," said Sam and went to sleep on the bench.

Pupils draw a line under the words in the 'ch' family.

New word: they

Read the Grandad Bill Story

Grandad Bill and the twins crept along the street to the shop but it felt much too hard with just socks on. They sat on a bench in the boot shop and Holly had her chin on her hand. Harry held his cheek and Grandad held his chest.

"Can I help?" said the boot shop man.

"Yes please," said Grandad. "It's not much. We just need boots. Boots for Holly, for Harry and for me."

"Red boots, please," said Holly.

"Green boots, please," said Harry.

"Black boots for me," said Grandad Bill.

"I will check the boots," said the shop man and went to the back of the shop.

Pupils identify and write 4 words beginning with 'ch'.

Teaching Points
(a) Draw attention to 'ck' and 'en' in chicken.
(b) Discuss two meanings of cheek.
(c) Feel 'n' in lunch, bench and crunch.
(d) Remind about speech marks.

th

thing	**th**em
clo**th**	**th**is
mo**th**	**th**at
fro**th**	**th**en
thrush	**th**ud
the	**th**ump

Dictate the Sam and the Tramp Story

As he slept, a moth struck Sam's cheek. He fell off the bench with a thud. The tramp sprang to help him. The bench shot up and sent them into the pond. Splash!

They stood up. Green weed clung to them.

Pupils draw a line under the words in the 'th' family.

Read the Grandad Bill Story

Grandad Bill and the West twins sat on the bench until Holly saw the shop man with three sets of boots.

"I am sorry," said the man. "I have no red, and no black boots, just green boots." The boots fell with a thud on the bench.

"That's sad," said Grandad. "Green boots are not the thing for a Grandad."

"That's sad," said Holly and she began to thump the bench. Then she got up and ran from the shop.

"Stop," said Grandad. "Rush off and get her back, Harry."

Harry ran from the shop in his socks.

Pupils identify and write 4 words beginning with 'th'.

Teaching Points

(a) Discuss 's (Sam's).
(b) Remind of 'ck' in 'struck'
(c) Discuss 'voicing' in 'them' and 'non-voicing' in 'thing'.

a e

c **a** m **e**	s **a** m **e**
g **a** v **e**	s h **a** k **e**
b r **a** v **e**	t **a** k **e**
b l **a** m **e**	t **a** s t **e**
n **a** m **e**	w **a** v **e**
m **a** k **e**	f **a** c **e**
s **a** f **e**	s c **a** l **e**

Dictate the Sam and the Tramp Story

The tramp gave a shake and came to the bank. Sam gave a shake and made such big waves that the ducks swam off. He was stuck in the mud. The tramp came to take his arm. Soon they were safe on the bank.

Pupils draw a line under the words in the 'a-e' family.

New words: was, were

Read the Grandad Bill story

Harry did not blame Holly. It was no good for them to have the same green boots. He ran on until he came back to the yard. Holly stood on the plank with the man from the coffee bar.

"Take my boots from the tar, please," she said with a sad look on her face. "Shake them free."

The man began to shake the red boots. The wet tar began to make waves. He gave a big shake and the boots were free. Oo-oops! The boots were free but the brave man was in the tar.

Pupils identify and write 4 words in the 'a-e' family.

Teaching Points

(a) Draw attention to soft 'c' in face, 'e' has two jobs – changing ă to ā and making 'c' sound 's'.

(b) Discuss – letters have names as well as sounds. 'e' makes 'a' say its name.

i_e

r **i** d **e**		t **i e**
d r **i** v **e**		w **i** p **e**
h **i** d **e**		**i** c **e**
m **i** l **e**		n **i** c **e**
s m **i** l **e**		s l **i** c **e**
p **i e**		s l **i** d **e**

Dictate the Sam and the Tramp Story

With a smile, Sam began to wipe his face with his tie. The wet tramp went to hide in the shed.

"Come on," said Sam. "Let's ride on the bus to my wife and have a nice, slice of pie."

Pupils draw a line under the words in the 'i-e' family.

New words: began, come, have

Read the Grandad Bill Story

Holly and Harry gave the coffee bar man a tug and he began to slide across the wet tar to the plank. As he got up he began to wipe his hands on his tie.

Harry gave a smile and said, "You must hide from your wife. She will not like the wet tar."

The coffee bar man said to Holly and Harry, "No, it is Grandad Bill who must hide! I blame him for the mess with the tar and Sad Gran will blame him for the bump in the van."

Harry said, "Take the boots, Holly, and wipe the tar off if you can. They look black, not red boots."

Pupils identify and write 4 words in the 'i-e' family.

Teaching Points

(a) Draw attention to 'pie' and 'tie' – no other letter between 'i' and 'e'.
(b) In ice, nice, and slice – 'e' has two jobs.
(c) Discuss 's in 'Let's' (Let us).

n **o** t **e**	d r **o** v **e**
s t **o** n **e**	r **o** d **e**
c l **o** s **e**	h **o** m **e**
c l **o** s **e** d	h **o** p **e**
o p **e** n	r **o** s **e**

Dictate the Sam and the Tramp Story

The two wet men closed the shed and rode home on the bus. Sam took his wife a red rose in a stone jar.

"I hope my wife will be at home," he said. "I will give her the rose and hope she will not be cross."

Pupils draw a line under the words in the 'o-e' family.

New words: two, her, give

Read the Grandad Bill Story

The West twins went back to the boot shop.

Grandad rose from the bench as they went in. He had green boots on. "I hope Harry, that you will have green boots," he said.

"Oh, yes," said Harry and began to rub his big toe. Holly looked at her boots and said, "My red boots are black. I will go home and get the tar off."

The boot shop man gave his nose a rub and said. "I hope you get the tar off, but I think it will be hard. We close at six o'clock, if you do need to get green boots."

They left the shop and rode home in Sad Gran's van.

Pupils identify and write 4 words in the 'o-e' family.

Teaching Points

(a) Draw attention to position of 'e' in 'closed' and 'open'.
(b) Discuss again letter names/sounds.
(c) Check that all pupils can sequence the alphabet orally.

b l **u e**	f l **u** t **e**
g l **u e**	t **u** n **e**
c l **u e**	**u** s **e**
t r **u e**	e x c **u** s **e**

Dictate the Sam and the Tramp Story

The two men came to the garden gate. Sam thinks of an excuse to use. It is true that they are very wet, after they fell in the pond.

"You take her the rose and I'll sing her a sweet tune on my flute," says the tramp.

Pupils draw a line under the words in the 'u-e' family.

New word: very

Read the Grandad Bill Story

When they got to Sad Gran's, Grandad Bill went with them as they opened the gate. "I'll tell Sad Gran," he said. "I got you into the tar. It's true, not just an excuse."

"Thanks, Grandad," said the West twins and went inside.

"Hello, Sad Gran," said the twins.

"Hello," said Sad Gran. "Did you go to the bank for the cash?"

Then she saw Holly's boots. Grandad gave her a clue. "I hope you like my green boots – and Harry's too."

"Yes," said Sad Gran. "But what did Holly use her boots for? Her boots are black."

"I will not make an excuse," said Grandad. "I took the twins into wet tar."

"Wet tar?" said Sad Gran. "Is that true?" She gave the twins a cross look.

Pupils identify and write 4 words in the 'u-e' family.

Teaching Points
(a) Draw attention to blue, glue, clue and true. No other letter between u/e.
(b) Discuss ex/cuse.
(c) Discuss I'll (I will).

ai

r **ai** n	a fr **ai** d
p **ai** n	ch **ai** n
p **ai** n t	n **ai** l
w **ai** t	s **ai** l
a g **ai** n	e x p l **ai** n

Dictate the Sam and the Tramp Story

The tramp and Sam are very wet, because they fell in the pond. Sam looks afraid, as he creeps inside to explain to his wife.

The tramp waits at the gate with his bag and his flute.

"I am very wet," says Sam to his wife, "but not from rain. I sat in the pond again."

His wife has a pot of paint and a paint brush in her hands. A look of pain is on her face.

Pupils draw a line under the words in the 'ai' family.

Words to practise: says, ones

Read the Grandad Bill Story

"Sit and explain, Grandad Bill," said Sad Gran.

Grandad sat on a bench and began to explain the true story.

He was afraid, but she began to smile.

"Oh, Grandad," she said. "I can see the story is true. Let's look at the boots."

She gave a long look at the green boots. "Fine," she said.

Then again, she gave a long look at Holly's black boots. She took a cloth and gave them a rub. "I'm afraid, Grandad," she said. "It's no good. Holly must have more boots."

Grandad explained that the shop had green boots, but no red ones.

"You must go back again to the shop and get green boots, Holly," said Sad Gran.

Pupils identify and write 3 words in the 'ai' family.

Teaching Points

(a) Discuss 'again' – in this family, although we usually say 'agen'. Do not write 'agen' – only discuss sound.
(b) Discuss ex/plain, a/fraid. Before dictation discuss in/side.
(c) Listen to 'brush' and discuss sounds before dictation.

oa

r **o a** d	g **o a** t
s **o a** p	m **o a** n
s **o a** k	**o a** k
c **o a** l	r **o a** s t
g **o a** l	t **o a** d

Dictate the Sam and the Tramp Story

The tramp stands at the gate with his flute. He is still soaking wet. His hands and face are as black as coal. He has not used soap for many weeks.

He sees that Sam's wife looks cross. With a soft moan, he grabs his bag and runs back to the road.

Pupils draw a line under the words in the 'oa' family.

New words: are, many

Read the Grandad Bill Story

Holly was moaning as they went along the road to the shop to get the green boots. "Green boots will not look nice with my red coat, Grandad," she said.

"Green boots do not look nice with my black coat," said Grandad. "But we must have boots."

It began to rain hard and they got soaking wet. They went across the road to the boot shop.

"My goodness," said the shop man. "You are soaking wet. It must be raining very hard. Take off your coats."

"We have come back for more green boots for Holly," said Grandad.

Holly gave a groan.

Pupils identify and write 2 words in the 'oa' family ending in 'ing'.

Teaching Points

(a) Discuss and feel – 'ing' as in 'ring', 'string', 'soaking'.
(b) Discuss, with pictures, the toad.
(c) Discuss 's – man's wife.
(d) Discuss 'used' (use/used), before dictation

ir

g**ir**l
f**ir** tree
st**ir**
s**ir**

d**ir**ty
th**ir**ty
th**ir**sty
c**ir**cus

Dictate the Sam and the Tramp Story

The tramp felt dirty and thirsty. He stood by a fir tree for a rest. A girl rode up to him on a bike.

"Excuse me sir," she said, "are you the tramp with the flute? Please come home for a nice, slice of pie."

The dirty, thirsty tramp took his bag and his flute, then he went back with the girl.

Pupils draw a line under the words in the 'ir' family.

New words: me, please

Read the Grandad Bill Story

Grandad sat and waited and gave his dirty shirt a rub. "I think it's tar," he said.

Holly looked at her skirt. She was too cross to look at Grandad's shirt. The shop man came back and she began to smile. In his hands he had red boots. "If they fit the girl," he said, "she can have red boots."

"Oh sir," said Holly, "they will fit." She put her feet into the red boots. There was a pain in her big toe.

"Do they fit?" said Grandad.

"Oh yes," said Holly, but it was not true. She felt the pain again.

"Take them off," said Grandad. "They will get dirty in the rain."

"No," said Holly. "I will keep them on." She went into the street.

Pupils identify and write 4 words in the 'ir' family.

Teaching Points

(a) Draw attention to 'y' sounding 'ee', in dirty, thirty, and thirsty.

(b) Discuss cir/cus. 'c' sounds 's' when followed by 'i' and 'k' when followed by 'u'.

(c) Discuss 'rode', in 'silent e' family, before dictation.

(d) Discuss ? (question mark)

ou (ow)

h**ou**se	ab**ou**t
m**ou**th	c**ou**nt
s**ou**nd	gr**ou**nd
r**ou**nd	p**ou**nd
sh**ou**t	**ou**tside
sh**ou**ted	pr**ou**d
al**ou**d	

Dictate the Sam and the Tramp Story

In about thirty seconds, the girl and the tramp stood outside the house. They went round the back. Sam and his wife were waiting for them.

"My name is Sue and he is Sam," said his wife. "What is your name?"

The tramp opened his mouth but no sound came out.

Pupils draw a line under the words in the 'ou' family.

New words: what, your

Read the Grandad Bill Story

Grandad left Holly outside Sad Gran's house and went off in the van. He had a big, round sweet in his mouth, so he did not sing.

As he went round the bend, a dog ran into the road. Grandad gave a loud toot on his horn and put on his brakes. The dog ran off and Grandad shouted at him.

But, the sound of the horn went on. "Toot – toot – toot." It was very loud. As Grandad drove about, the horn did not stop. "Toot – toot – toot."

Men in cars shouted at Grandad and waved at the van. But the sound of the horn went on.

Pupils identify and write 2 words ending in 'ound' and 2 more words with 'out' in them.

Teaching Points
(a) Draw attention to final 'e' on house.
(b) Discuss 'ed' on shouted.
(c) Before dictation, remind of 'closed', 'open'. Discuss 'opened'.
(d) Discuss Sue – link with blue, glue, etc.
(e) Discuss 'seconds' – passing of time – and the spelling.
(f) Remind pupils of ? (question mark).

ea (ee)

t e a	s c r e a m
t e a c h	f l e a
p e a c h	r e a d
e a c h	p l e a s e
c r e a m	s p e a k

Dictate the Sam and the Tramp Story

    Sue got out four cups and made the tea. She gave them each a slice of peach pie with cream.

    Then she gave a cup of tea to the tramp. A flea jumped out of his coat.

    She let out a scream and dropped the hot tea on the tramp's foot.

Pupils draw a line under the words in the 'ea' family.

New word: four

Read the Grandad Bill Story

    Grandad drove home. He left the van in the drive but the sound of the horn still went on. "Toot – toot. Toot – toot."

    "I shall scream at that horn," said Sad Gran.

    They each had a peach with cream to eat and tea to drink.

    "I think I shall scream too," said Grandad. "First the bad cat, then the van, then the tar, then the boots and that horn."

    A man came to the gate and shouted. "Please will you stop that horn."

    Grandad got up from his seat. He left his cup of tea, his peach and cream and went out to speak to the man.

Pupils identify and write 3 words about food or drink in the 'ea' family.

Teaching Points

(a) Draw attention to final 'e' on please.
(b) Before dictation discuss 's – tramp's foot.
(c) Discuss 'pp' in dropped. Rule is – double the consonant to keep the vowel short.
(d) Remind of 'ed' ending – jumped and dropped.

ay

d**ay**	sw**ay**
tod**ay**	h**ay**
Tuesd**ay**	tr**ay**
Wednesd**ay**	str**ay**
m**ay**	railw**ay**
st**ay**	

Dictate the Sam and the Tramp Story

The tramp gave a shout. The flea hopped on the tray and a stray cat jumped on the flea.

The stray cat missed the flea and landed on the peach pie. Sam looked at the mess and groaned. "It's not my day today."

"Go away and stay away," screamed Sue.

Pupils draw a line under the words in the 'ay' family.

New word: go

Read the Grandad Bill Story

As Grandad went out into the drive, he saw it was Sam at the gate. "Oh no," he groaned. "Not him. Not today."

"Toot – toot. Toot – toot," went the horn.

"The horn will not stop," said Grandad. "There is no way I can make it stop."

"This Tuesday has been a bad day for you, Grandad," said Sam. "Wednesday may be better, if we can stop that horn. Get out of the way."

"Toot – toot. Toot – toot," went the horn, as Sam got into the van.

Pupils identify and write 2 words ending in 'day'. Use capital letters.

Teaching Points
(a) Suggest children think of 'blue, Tuesday'.
(b) Discuss Wed/nes/day.
(c) Discuss a/way.
(d) Remind of 'ed' ending and doubling consonant to keep vowel short – 'hopped'.
(e) Teach 'it's' (it is). Remind of I'll (I will).

ing

take – tak**ing**
make – mak**ing**
slide – slid**ing**
shine – shin**ing**
joke – jok**ing**
hope – hop**ing**

(Take off 'e' and add 'ing')

Dictate the Sam and the Tramp Story

Tripping over the stray cat and sliding on the peach pie, Sam went outside. The tramp grabbed his flute and his bag and ran out too. He had been hoping that Sue was joking.

Sam stood by the gate. Taking the tramp's arm, he said, "Let's go and sleep in my shed."

Pupils draw a line under the words in the 'ing' family.

New words: too, over

Read the Grandad Bill Story

As Grandad stood waiting at the gate, Sad Gran came out.
"That horn will still not stop," said Grandad Bill. "I'm hoping Sam can mend it."
"You must be joking," said Sad Gran. "He'll not fit into the van."
Sam had his left leg and arm inside the van and was hoping to slide the rest of himself in. His chest gave a thump and a thud.
"It's stopping," shouted Grandad.
"The horn's stopped but I'm stuck," said Sam.

Pupils identify and write 4 'ing' words.

Teaching Points
(a) Discuss the rule – take off 'e' before adding 'ing'. Point out that these words are in 'silent e' family.
(b) Remind of doubling consonant to keep short vowel – grabbed, then 'pp' in tripping.
(c) Listen to long vowels (letters saying their own names). Listen to short vowels and link to key words.
(d) Discuss 'Let's' (Let us). Remind of it's and I'll.

ur

ch**ur**ch	p**ur**se
b**ur**nt	n**ur**se
c**ur**l	t**ur**nip
f**ur**	Th**ur**sday
p**ur**r	Sat**ur**day

Dictate the Sam and the Tramp Story

Sam and the tramp went by the churchyard. On the ground they found a big turnip and began to eat it.

"It is not as nice as peach pie," they moaned.

"Was that stray cat sent away?" asked the tramp.

"No. She likes the cat with its purr and its fur," said sad Sam.

Pupils draw a line under the words in the 'ur' family.

New word: asked

Read the Grandad Bill Story

The horn had stopped, but Sam was still curled up in the van. He began to twist and turn, but he was stuck.

A nurse stopped at the gate and said to Grandad Bill, "I'm glad that horn has stopped."

"The horn has stopped, but Sam is stuck," said Grandad Bill.

"Sam is much too fat," said the nurse and went along the road to church.

Sam was getting more and more red. He looked as if he was going to burst. "Get me out!" he said.

"Come on Grandad," said Harry West, who had come out. "You take his feet and I'll shake him from the back."

"Will it hurt?" asked Grandad.

"Hope not," said Sam, as Grandad Bill began to twist and turn his feet. Harry gave Sam's back a bang and a shake.

Pupils identify and write 4 words in the 'ur' family.

Teaching Points

(a) Draw attention to 'rr' or 'purr'.
(b) Draw attention to final 'e' on purse and nurse.
(c) Remind ? (question mark)
(d) Discuss 'its' – 'its purr', 'its fur' – they belong to the cat.

aw

aw f u l	p **aw**
s **aw**	s t r **aw**
l **aw**	y **aw** n
j **aw**	c r **aw** l
d **aw** n	

Dictate the Sam and the Tramp Story

Sam and Gus the tramp lay on some straw inside the shed by the pond. Gus gave a yawn and fell asleep. Sam felt awful and did not sleep until dawn.

As they both slept, the straw began to burn. The smoke woke Gus the tramp and he shook Sam.

"Wake up. Let's get out."

They began to crawl out as the shed burnt to the ground.

Pupils draw a line under the words in the 'aw' family.

New words: some, until, both

Read the Grandad Bill Story

Sam is stuck in Sad Gran's van. Harry West and Grandad Bill are trying to help Sam get out.

"This is awful," said Sam, as his jaw hit the back of the seat and his purse fell on the ground.

Harry saw the purse drop and let go of Sam's feet. He began to crawl about to collect the cash and notes from the lawn.

"Stop that Harry," shouted Grandad Bill. "Get off the lawn and we will grab Sam's feet again."

He gave Sam a big bang and Harry gave a tug. There was an awful ripping sound and Sam fell onto the drive. He rolled across onto the lawn.

Grandad Bill jumped out of the way and then he saw Sam's shirt. Some of the shirt was still on Sam, but some of it was still in the van.

Pupils identify and write 4 words with 'aw' in them.

Teaching Points

(a) Draw attention to one 'l' at the end of 'awful'.
(b) Discuss the dawn.
(c) Remind – let's (let us).

oi

o i l	t **o i** l e t
s p **o i** l	c h **o i** c e
s **o i** l	v **o i** c e
n **o i** s y	

Dictate the Sam and the Tramp Story

Sam filled a pail from the pond and wet the soil around the burnt shed. He was very noisy as he splashed in and out of the pond.

A voice said, "It is against the law to burn park sheds and spoil the ponds. I have no choice. Come with me."

Pupils draw a line under the words in the 'oi' family.

Read the Grandad Bill Story

Sam got up from the lawn and shook soil from himself. Grandad Bill looked hard at him and said, "I'm afraid we have spoiled your shirt, but you are out of the van."

Sam looked at his shirt. "My wife Sue will be cross," he said. "But the choice was not hard. It was me, or the shirt."

Harry was still crawling on the lawn and the drive picking up Sam's coins and notes. It was getting dark and he was picking up soil and stones.

Grandad Bill began to shout in a noisy voice. "Get up Harry. It is too dark to see. Sam can get his cash in the morning."

Pupils identify and write 4 words with 'oi' in them.

Teaching Points

(a) Draw attention to: 'e' in toilet; 'y' making ee sound on noisy; to final 'e' on 'choice' and 'voice' making 'c' soft.
(b) Discuss the person behind "the voice".
(c) Listen to 'filled' and 'splashed' – discuss ending.
(d) Discuss 'against' – reminding of 'ai' family and listening to 'st'.

er

riv**er**	ov**er**
thund**er**	driv**er**
numb**er**	partn**er**
nev**er**	sw**er**ve
ev**er**	k**er**b
und**er**	

Dictate the Sam and the Tramp Story

The policeman took Sam and Gus the tramp to the driver of the police car. They sat in the back and never spoke.

As the driver took the road over the river, it began to thunder and rain ever so hard.

The police car began to swerve. Then, with a crash, it hit the kerb. The police driver fell over.

Gus jumped out of the crashed car, but Sam was stuck.

Pupils draw a line under the words in the 'er' family.

New words: police, policeman, police car

Read the Grandad Bill Story

Grandad Bill went into the house and came back with Sad Gran and a number of shirts over his arm. "See if one of my shirts will fit you," he said.

Sam took every shirt in turn, but not one fitted him.

"You will never find a shirt for Sam," said Sad Gran. "He's too fat for your shirts."

Just then, a loud crash of thunder made them jump.

"I think I had better dash home with Harry and Holly before it rains hard," said Sam.

"You will never get home before it rains but Harry and Holly must go home," said Grandad Bill. So Harry and Holly went home in their boots and Sam went inside.

Pupils identify and write 5 words with 'er' in them.

Teaching Points

(a) Draw attention to final 'e' on 'swerve'.
(b) Discuss 'kerb' and relate it to kerb-drill, if desired.
(c) Discuss partners – choosing partners – doing things in pairs.
(d) Discuss storms – black clouds – thunder – lightning – heavy rain.
(e) Speculate on what the tramp will do – after the dictation.

all – al

a l l	*take off one 'l' to add 'k' or an ending*
f a l l	t a l k
h a l l	w a l k
t a l l	c h a l k
w a l l	a l w a y s
s m a l l	t a l k i n g
	w a l k i n g

Dictate the Sam and the Tramp Story

Gus wanted to run away. He was too small to help Sam and the tall policeman was hurt. But he began talking.

"Sit still Sam. I will help the policeman first."

He took the walkie-talkie from the seat and began to call in a small, thin voice.

"Calling all cars. Calling all cars. We have crashed in Riverside Road. Over."

Pupils draw a line under the words in the 'all - al' family.

New words: want, wanted

Word to practise: too

Read the Grandad Bill Story

Sam and Grandad Bill walked into the house. Sam stood in the hall and Grandad went to talk to Sad Gran. They were talking a long time. Sam sat on a small stool to wait. Soon, Grandad Bill was walking back into the hall.

"Please stay and have supper with us," he said.

As Grandad was talking, a cracking sound came from the small stool. Cr-ack! The stool broke and Sam fell with a crash against the wall in the hall.

Sad Gran came into the hall.

"Did you fall?" she said to Sam. Then she saw the bits of stool all over the hall.

Pupils identify and write 3 words with 'alk' in them and 4 words ending in 'all'.

Teaching Points
(a) Discuss – take off one 'l' when adding 'k' or an ending ('always').
(b) Discuss the walkie-talkie and point out 'ie' ending.
(c) Ask which family 'hurt' is in. Then which family 'first' is in.
(d) Break down River/side. Discuss capitals for names of roads.
(e) Make sure all children can write their own address. If not, use finger tracing method.

ea (e)

h **e a** d	sw **e a** t
h **e a** v y	s p r **e a** d
r **e a** d y	b r **e a** t h
r **e a** d	m **e a** n t
i n s t **e a** d	d r **e a** d f u l

Dictate the Sam and the Tramp Story

Gus took the policeman's head. It was heavy and he began to sweat. Then hundreds of police cars with flashing blue lamps and noisy hooters came rushing up. They spread out around the crashed car.

Sam and Gus looked dreadful. The tramp took a deep breath. "Sorry. Sorry," he shouted. "I only meant one."

Pupils draw a line under the words in the 'ea' (e) family.

New words: only, sorry

Words to practise: one, they, hundred

Read the Grandad Bill Story

"Sam you were too heavy for that stool," said Sad Gran and shook her head.

Sam was spread out in the hall. He took a deep breath and began to sweat.

"Come on Sam," said Grandad Bill. "You must get up. Are you ready?"

Grandad Bill and Sad Gran took Sam's arms to help him up. Sam took a deep breath again. Sweat was running down his face and he shook his head. "No," he said. "I'm not ready."

Just then, Sue, Sam's wife, came into the hall. "Sam," she said, "you look dreadful. What are you doing? You must come home."

Grandad Bill and Sue took Sam's hands. "One, two, three – Up," said Sue.

Pupils identify and write 5 words with 'ea (ē)' in them.

Teaching Points

(a) Remind 'y' making 'ee' sound on heavy and ready.
(b) Break down in/stead. Feel 'spr' (spread).
(c) Point out single 'l' on 'dreadful'.
(d) Discuss times when people take a deep breath.

ow

Dictate the Sam and the Tramp Story

Policemen began to crowd round the car. They saw the dirty tramp with the hurt policeman and frowned.

They saw how Sam was stuck in the back. The frowns turned to smiles and they began to laugh. Hundreds of policemen stood and laughed. The row drowned the noise of the hooters.

The hurt policeman opened his eyes and sat up. His eyebrows shot up.

"However did all the policemen in town get here?" he asked.

Pupils draw a line under the words in the 'ow' family.

New words: laugh, laughed, eye, here

Read the Grandad Bill Story

Grandad Bill and Sue gave a tug and Sad Gran gave a frown as Sam began to rise and then fell back down again.

She raised her eyebrows. "Come on, Sam," she said. "Get up however you like, but do not just spread yourself in Grandad's hall."

Sam frowned and began to turn round on the brown carpet. He felt dreadful and began to crawl out of the hall.

"Get up, Sam," said Grandad Bill. "It's no good crawling out of the house. You cannot crawl home across the town in this rain."

Pupils identify and write 4 words ending in 'own'.

Teaching Points

(a) Discuss 'ed' endings.
(b) Break down how/ever.
(c) Teach 'eye', before 'eyebrow'.
(d) Discuss which family 'dirty', 'hurt' and 'round' belong to *before* dictation.

igh

l i g h t	f r i g h t e n
n i g h t	f r i g h t e n e d
t o n i g h t	f i g h t
m i d n i g h t	h i g h
r i g h t	s i g h
b r i g h t	s i g h t
f r i g h t	m i g h t

Dictate the Sam and the Tramp Story

Sam and Gus felt frightened. The sight of all those policemen standing in the bright moonlight made them feel ill. In a high thin voice the tramp said, "I called them on your walkie-talkie."

The church clock struck midnight and Gus jumped with fright. He jumped out of the car and ran and ran. He ran away from the laughing policemen and out of sight of Sam who was still stuck in the car.

Pupils draw a line under the words in the 'igh' family.

New word: who

Word to practise: your

Read the Grandad Bill Story

It was dark now, but there was a bright light outside. Sam was on the steps outside and gave a big sigh.

"Get up, Sam," said Sue. "You look such a sight."

"I will," said Sam, "if I can get my feet right." His feet were now out of sight.

A big voice gave a shout, "What's going on in Grandad Bill's house tonight?"

Sam was so frightened that he jumped up and stood in the bright light on the drive. Sue and Grandad Bill began to laugh.

"I'm glad that policeman came along tonight, Sam, to frighten you," said Grandad Bill. "You might have been stuck on my steps all night."

Pupils identify and write 5 words in the 'igh' family.

Teaching Points

(a) Discuss the building of 'fright' to 'frightened', also of 'night' to 'tonight' and 'midnight'.
(b) Discuss the meanings of 'right'.
   (i) left/right – through activities check that no children have left/right confusion.
   (ii) right/wrong.
(c) Before dictation listen to 'feel ill'. Discuss the sounds and how they are written. Link 'still' with 'ill'.

a (ar)

cl**a**ss	l**a**st
cl**a**ssroom	bl**a**st
gr**a**ss	f**a**st
gl**a**ss	p**a**th
p**a**ss	f**a**ther
ask	r**a**ther
asked	c**a**n't
after	

Dictate the Sam and the Tramp Story

Policemen jumped into their cars to chase Gus. They flashed their blue lights and gave a blast on their hooters. But he was too fast and ran down the path to the long grass. Two policemen ran after him.

"Why didn't you run away?" a policeman asked Sam.

"I can't," groaned Sam. "I'm rather stuck and I can't run fast anyway."

Pupils draw a line under the words in the 'a' (ar) family.

New words: why, their, anyway

Word to practise: two

Read the Grandad Bill Story

The big policeman walked up the path and across the grass with a flash light. "What have you been up to?" he asked. Sam stood next to the policeman on the grass and gave a sigh.

He spoke at last. "I was rather stuck in Grandad Bill's hall," he said.

"Have you lost your shirt in a blast too?" asked the policeman and gave Sam's torn shirt a rather hard tug. The rest of the shirt came off in his hands.

"You had better go home fast," he said and stood back to let Sam pass.

"Not too fast Sam," said Sue and came running down the path with a pile of clean shirts.

Pupils identify and write 4 words in the 'a' family.

Teaching Points

(a) Discuss abbreviations used in colloquial English. Can't (cannot), I'll (I will), I'm (I am), didn't (did not), it's (it is).

(b) Discuss 'too' ('too fast') – revision.

(c) Remind – ? (question mark)

o (u)

List A:		List B:	
m **o** t h e r		c **o** m e	
b r **o** t h e r		s **o** m e	
s **o** n		d **o** n e	
o t h e r		g l **o** v e	
o v e n		l **o** v e	
w **o** n		m **o** n e y	
M **o** n d a y		m **o** n k e y	
f r **o** n t		n **o** n e	
L **o** n d o n			
m **o** n t h			

Dictate the Sam and the Tramp Story

Some other policemen came to help Sam. Some tugged from the front and some from the back. At last they won and Sam was out of the car.

"That's my brother," said a short, fat policeman. "Sam, what have you done?"

Sam began to explain and the other policemen got quietly into their cars and drove off into the dark night.

Pupils draw a line under the words in the 'o' (u) family.

New word: quietly

Read the Grandad Bill Story

Sue saw that the policeman was Sam's brother, Bob. "Come on Sam," she said. "Pick another shirt and let's go home."

"None of these shirts will fit," groaned Sam.

"One of them must," said Sue. Sam tugged hard at a blue shirt.

"Stop, Sam," shouted Sue, but she was too late. As Sam tugged, all the other clean shirts fell onto the lawn in front of Bob the policeman. "Look what you've done," shouted Sue.

"Oh how awful," groaned Sam.

"Come on love," said Bob to Sue. "Let's pick up the shirts and see what harm has been done."

Pupils identify and write 4 words in the 'o (u)' family.

Teaching Points
(a) List A is largely revision of words learned in Introductory List. Revise this one day and introduce List B the next day.
(b) Discuss 'y' saying 'ee' in 'money' and 'monkey'.
(c) Remind of capital letters for days of the week and places.
(d) Discuss meaning of 'won'.
(e) Discuss 'that's' (that is).
(f) Remind that 'explain' is in the 'rain family'.
(g) Remind – 2 consonants needed to keep vowel short – 'tugged'.

y (i)

cry – crying	spy – spying
fly – flying	my – myself
fry – frying	sky
try – trying	shy
dry – drying	why

Dictate the Sam and the Tramp story

As Sam was trying to explain, Gus crept back along the path from the long grass. He had been spying, but was too shy to ask why the other policemen had gone.

"Come home with me," said brother Bob. "My wife is away, so I shall be frying fish for myself."

The two brothers walked off. The shy tramp hid again in the long grass. He was by himself and felt like crying.

Pupils draw a line under the words in the 'y' (i) family.

New word: gone

Word to practise: two

Read the Grandad Bill Story

Grandad Bill, Sad Gran, Sue and policeman Bob, crawled about on the wet lawn in the dark, trying to pick up the shirts. "They'll all need drying," said Sue.

Sam was trying on the blue shirt. He had his arms in, but the shirt did not reach round his chest. "I'm not very pleased with myself," he said. "I think I am getting fatter."

The others stood up to look. Sad Gran gave a cry. "Oh Sam," she said, spying his chest peeping out from the shirt. "You must stop frying your chicken and chips and try to slim."

Sue was looking at the wet, dirty shirts and trying not to be cross. "I'm going home," she said and went flying out of the gate.

Pupils identify and write 4 words ending in 'ying'.

Teaching Points

(a) Remind of the words learned in Introductory List and show the 'ing' added.
(b) Link 'why' with other question words, already covered in basic words – 'who', 'what' – plus 'when'.
(c) Remind that 'again' is in the 'rain' family.
(d) After dictation ask for comments on "Come home." (Look the same – sound different – different families).

ow (o)

sn**o**w	wind**o**w
gr**o**w	yell**o**w
l**o**w	pill**o**w
sl**o**w	foll**o**w
bl**o**w	arr**o**w
sh**o**w	marr**o**w
m**o**w	tomorr**o**w
r**o**w	elb**o**w
thr**o**w	bel**o**w

Dictate the Sam and the Tramp Story

Gus began to follow the path back to the pond. He hurt his elbow on a yellow twig which was growing low. He felt very unhappy tonight. Tomorrow things might be better. Then there was a shout from below. Gus looked beyond the row of trees. It was the policeman with the big voice.

"Follow me," he said.

Pupils draw a line under the words in the 'ow' (o) family.

New word: which

Word to practise: very

Read the Grandad Bill Story

Sam slowly began to follow Sue out of the gate. He gave his blue shirt a tug, so as not to show his chest. When he was standing in the road, he turned and said, "I'll be back tomorrow, Grandad. I'll mend that stool, so do not throw it away."

"He did not fly off like Sue," said policeman Bob.

"No, he is always rather slow," said Grandad Bill.

Bob the policeman began to follow Sam across the lawn to the gate. His feet felt something. He bent down and picked up a dirty yellow shirt.

He got to the gate and his feet felt something again. He bent down and picked up another yellow shirt.

He turned back to the house. "If I throw these shirts to you, Grandad Bill, you can give them to Sam tomorrow morning," he called.

Pupils identify and write 4 words with 'ow' (o) in them.

Teaching Points

(a) Remind of 'ow' words learned in Introductory List. Move on to new ones – and 'ow' ending.

(b) Point out double consonants to keep vowels short.

(c) Point out single 'l' in be/low. Then introduce be/gan and be/yond, which will be met in dictation.

(d) Discuss double consonants/short vowels to be met in dictation – 'unhappy', 'better'.

ew

n e w	d r e w
f e w	f l e w
c h e w	s c r e w
g r e w	t h r e w
b l e w	k n e w

Dictate the Sam and the Tramp Story

In a few seconds Gus stood with the policeman. The wind blew and the sky grew dark. The policeman threw the tramp some chewing gum. "Chew that," he said.

Gus followed the policeman along the path. The stones hurt his feet. He must get some new boots, but he had no money.

It began to rain hard. Gus was wet. The policeman looked at him. "I think you need a hot bath and a few new things," he said.

Pupils draw a line under the words in the 'ew' family.

Read the Grandad Bill Story

Policeman Bob threw the dirty yellow shirts to Grandad Bill. They hit the wall in the hall and then fell onto the carpet. Sad Gran drew a deep breath. "I knew it!" she said. "Those men! First the stool and now the wall."

"We will get a new stool and some fresh paint," said Grandad Bill. "It will only cost a few pounds."

Sad Gran's face grew sad. "We will have no money left," she said. "First the van, then the boots, then Sam's shirt, then the stool and now the wall. I knew this was a bad day."

Pupils identify and write 4 words with 'ew' in them.

Teaching Points

(a) Discuss new things – books, toys, clothes, etc.
(b) Discuss 'flew' (the bird flew away) and 'threw' (he threw the ball across the room).
(c) Discuss ending on 'followed' and divide a/long.
(d) Remind of 'money' family and 'y' ending.

tion

ac**tion**	invita**tion**
sta**tion**	decora**tion**
rela**tion**	direc**tion**
conversa**tion**	correc**tion**

Dictate the Sam and the Tramp Story

Gus the tramp felt frightened as he followed the policeman into the police station.

The policeman had a conversation with some other men and then said, "Now we are ready for action." He gave Gus directions to the bathroom. "Take this soap. Have a nice, hot bath and I will visit my relations and get you some new things."

Pupils draw a line under the words in the 'tion' family.

Read the Grandad Bill Story

In the morning, Grandad Bill walked down to the station. When he got back, Sad Gran was having a conversation at the gate with the West twins.

"Hello Grandad Bill," said Harry and Holly. "Here is an invitation to tea on Sunday. All of the relations are coming."

"All of them?" asked Grandad with a smile.

"Yes – all," said the twins. "It's our birthday."

"We are just going to the shop to get decorations for the birthday cake," said Holly.

They went off in the direction of the shop. Sam came along from the other direction on his blue bike. He had a bag of tools on the back.

"Here comes the action man," said Grandad Bill with a smile.

"I want no action from Sam in my house," said Sad Gran.

Pupils identify and write 4 words ending in 'tion'.

Teaching Points

(a) Discuss 'tion' as the usual ending when 'shun' is heard.
(b) Discuss relations – brothers, sisters, aunts, uncles, etc.
(c) Give them five minutes to have a conversation with a child of their choice – then report it.
(d) Discuss invitations – birthday, wedding, etc.
(e) Draw attention to double 'rr' in correction and discuss meaning.

oy

b o y
t o y
j o y

e n j o y
e n j o y e d
a n n o y
a n n o y e d

Dictate the Sam and the Tramp Story

Gus enjoyed his bath. He remembered when he was a boy and played with his toys in the bath. Now as he grew cleaner, the bath became blacker and blacker. "The policemen will be annoyed if the bath is so dirty," he said to himself. He got out of the bath to look for a cloth, but there was none.

As he walked around the bathroom, he left pools of water everywhere. He looked at the pools and he looked at the dirty bath. He was frightened and wished he was a boy again, playing with his toys in the bath.

Pupils draw a line under the words in the 'oy' family.

New words: there, everywhere, water

Read the Grandad Bill Story

Sad Gran looked annoyed as Sam got off his blue bike with the tools. "Good morning," he said. "I shall enjoy mending your stool."

"The stool is fine, Sam," said Grandad Bill as he saw the annoyed look on Sad Gran's face.

Sam ran in the direction of the house, like a boy going after a new toy. "Action, Grandad," said his wife in a soft voice. "Do not let Sam get close to that stool with his tools." Grandad Bill followed Sam along the path and put his hand on Sam's elbow.

"Oh Sam," he said. "Before you go into the hall, come and see the toy train I've got for Harry and Holly. It is their birthday."

"I shall enjoy playing with a toy train more than mending a stool," said Sam with a laugh.

Pupils identify and write 4 words with 'oy' in them.

Teaching Points
(a) Point out 'nn' in 'annoy' and 'ed' on 'annoyed' and 'enjoyed'.
(b) Link remembered with 'er' family and get children to feel syllables – re/mem/ber/ed.
(c) Link 'er' ending also to 'cleaner' and 'blacker'.
(d) Remind of o = u family – 'none'.

au

s **au** c e	**au** t u m n
s **au** c e p a n	h **au** n t e d
s **au** c e r	f **au** l t
Au g u s t	**au** t o m a t i c

*Looks the same – sounds different – s**au**sage*

Dictate the Sam and the Tramp Story

There was a loud shout from outside. "Have you had a nice bath?"

"Yes, thank you, but I've made rather a mess," said Gus the tramp.

A brown bag was dropped into the bathroom and splashed in a pool. "Don't worry. Get dressed, then come and have sausages and beans with tomato sauce. There is some hot milk in the saucepan, if you can drink from a saucer. We've just smashed all the cups."

Pupils draw a line under the words in the 'au' family.

Read the Grandad Bill Story

Grandad Bill and Sam went into the garden shed. "It may be August," said Sam, "but the sun's not very hot."

"More like autumn," said Grandad. "Now, let's look at the toy train." He lifted a saucepan off a box.

"Look inside the box," he said to Sam. Like two boys, they looked inside the box.

"Is it automatic?" asked Sam.

"Well, it's electric," said Grandad. "You don't need a key." They lifted the rails out of the box.

"Let's make up the rails in the shed to see if there are any faults," said Sam. Sam sat down with the rails in the dirt and mess of the shed. There was no room left for Grandad.

"I'll go into the house and get some sausages to eat," he said.

Pupils identify and write 4 words with 'au' in them.

Teaching Points

(a) Remind 'e' making 'c' sound on 'sauce' etc.
(b) Remind of capital letter for month.
(c) Point out 'n' on autumn.
(d) Discuss ways of saying 'fault' (folt).
(e) Divide au/to/mat/ic and discuss automatic things.
(f) Introduce 'sausage' as part of this family, even though it sounds different.
(g) Discuss abbreviations – I've (I have), Don't (do not), We've (we have).
(h) Link 'worry' to 'mother' family and tomato to 'path' family.

ī

f **i** n d	b l **i** n d
k **i** n d	b e h **i** n d
m **i** n d	l **i** o n
p **i** n t	c h **i** l d
t **i** d y	F r **i** d a y
t **i** n y	

Dictate the Sam and the Tramp Story

Gus looked in the brown bag to see the things the kind policeman had given him. He did not mind what kind of new shirt or trousers he had, as long as they were clean and tidy.

He looked in the tiny mirror behind the shower, but he could only see the top of his head. He went out to the policemen. They smiled to see the tramp in a blue shirt, green trousers and new, brown boots.

He blushed and said in a thin, high voice, "I could not find a cloth to tidy the bathroom. I'm afraid I've left an awful mess behind me."

Pupils draw a line under the words in the 'ī' family.

New words: give, given, could

Word to practise: only

Read the Grandad Bill Story

Grandad Bill went to cook some sausages but he could not find any. He looked behind the tomato sauce.

"I wish my wife was tidy," he said. "Then perhaps I could find some sausages."

He picked up a pint of milk. It was wet and slipped out of his hands. Crash! Milk and glass were everywhere.

"Grandad Bill," a child's voice said. "What an awful mess." Grandad turned to find Holly West peeping at him. She had her new red boots on.

"I was looking for some sausages to cook," said Grandad Bill.

"Sad Gran has gone shopping to get some," said Holly.

"Quick," said Grandad. "She mustn't come home and find this mess. Will you help me tidy up, Holly?"

Holly West took a tiny mop and Grandad took a big broom. They began to tidy up the glass and milk.

Pupils identify and write 4 words in the 'ī' family.

Teaching Points

(a) Look at the two families in 'trousers'. Add word to both word family lists.
(b) Repeat with 'shower' and also add to 'sh' list.
(c) Talk about 'rr' in mirror.
(d) Feel sounds in bl-u-sh-ed. Talk about blushing and why.

ear

h **ear**	f **ear**
ear	b **ear** d
d **ear**	t **ear** s
n **ear**	y **ear**
n **ear** l y	

Dictate the Sam and the Tramp Story

Gus the tramp has had a bath. He is dressed in a blue shirt, green trousers and new, brown boots. He sat down near the kind policeman to eat his sausages and beans with tomato sauce. They gave him a saucer of hot milk from the saucepan. He could not drink it. His long beard flopped into the saucer.

"Oh dear," he said and tears came into his eyes. His beard had not been cut for years.

The kind policeman came near him with some scissors. "Have no fears," he said. "We'd better cut that beard."

Pupils draw a line under the words in the 'ear' family.

New words: of, scissors

Words to practise: could, eyes

Read the Grandad Bill Story

Grandad Bill and Holly West did not hear the gate open. They had nearly finished clearing up when a voice made them jump "Oh dear, what have you been up to now?" It was Sad Gran back from the shops. Grandad Bill began to stroke his beard and Holly West rubbed her ear.

"I dropped the milk," said Grandad, "and Holly was very kind. She helped me to clear up."

"You are a dear, Holly," said Sad Gran. "Take off your boots and have a cup of tea with us."

"My boots are stuck on," said Holly. She was nearly in tears. "I can't get them off."

"Not at all?" asked Grandad Bill. "What about when you go to bed?"

"I keep them on in bed," said Holly and the tears began to fall.

"I'll get Sam from the shed," said Grandad. "We'll soon get them off with his tools."

Pupils identify and write 4 words with 'ear' in them.

Teaching Points
(a) Remind that 'sausages' is in the 'au' family like sauce and saucer. Make children think about 'tomato'.
(b) Listen to 'flopped'. Ask how many 'p's and why. How many 't's in better?
(c) Abbreviation – we'd (we had).
(d) Look at three tricky bits in sc-i-ss-or-s. Then finger trace as for basic words.
(e) Talk about 'oh' as in 'oh dear', 'oh really', 'oh well', etc.

air

h **air**	ch **air**
h **air** y	st **air** s
f **air**	up st **air** s
p **air**	d o w n st **air** s
r e p **air**	f **air** y
air	

Dictate the Sam and the Tramp Story

The policeman took Gus upstairs to a room with a big mirror. He sat on a chair and the policeman began to cut the beard with a pair of scissors. He cut until the beard was short and smart. "I think you should cut my hair too," said the tramp.

The policeman cut Gus's fair hair short round the ears. Then he cut the hair at the back and across the forehead. "Now come downstairs and show yourself," said the policeman.

Gus got up from the chair and the pair went back down the stairs.

Pupils draw a line under the words in the 'air' family.

New word: should

Read the Grandad Bill Story

Holly West sat on a chair and waited. Sad Gran went upstairs and Grandad Bill went to the shed. Holly looked at the pair of red boots stuck on her feet and began to stroke her long fair hair. Her tears began to fall again. As Sad Gran came downstairs, Grandad Bill and Sam came in from the shed. "I came to repair a stool," said Sam, "not to take off boots. My tools may not be right."

"Now, Holly," said Grandad, "hold tight to the chair."

"Please don't tug, Grandad," said Holly. "My legs and feet hurt so much."

"Now you men, get out of my way," said Sad Gran. In her hand she had a big pair of scissors. "Keep very still, Holly," she said and very slowly began to cut the pair of new, red boots.

Pupils identify and write 4 words with 'air' in them.

Teaching Points

(a) Discuss fairs. Also fair (colour) and "It's not fair".
(b) Link 'pair' with – "repair a pair of shoes".
(c) Discuss 'forehead' – pronunciation (fo/red) and spelling 'fore' (meaning front) and 'head'. Link with fore-legs and fore/aft (boats).
(d) Remind of 'too' (as well).

ou (ŭ)

t**ou**ch	c**ou**ntry
t**ou**ched	tr**ou**ble
y**ou**ng	d**ou**ble
y**ou**nger	c**ou**ple

Dictate the Sam and the Tramp Story

The couple went back into the downstairs room. The policemen were still eating sausages and beans. They looked up and said to the tramp, "You look much younger."

Gus touched his smart hair and beard with his hands and smiled. "This kind policeman took a lot of trouble. He is a good barber."

Pupils draw a line under the words in the 'ou' family that sound like 'touch'.

Word to practise: were

Read the Grandad Bill Story

Grandad Bill, Sam and Holly West looked at the big scissors as Sad Gran cut the new red boots with no trouble at all. After a couple more cuts, one foot was free and Holly touched her toes. She looked very happy. As Sad Gran began to cut the other boot, there was a sound in the hall.

"Holly, Holly. Are you here?" It was Harry. He had come to find her. He looked at the new pair of red boots on the carpet and his eyes nearly popped out of his head. "There will be trouble when we get home," he said. "What will Mum say?"

"Now young man," said Grandad Bill and he touched the top of Harry's head. "Those boots have been a trouble to Holly for nearly a week. You can't sleep in boots."

"She should have had green boots," said Harry and began to pick up the bits of red boots.

Holly touched her feet and began to wiggle her toes.

Pupils identify and write 3 words with 'ou' (ŭ) in them.

Teaching Points
(a) Link 'couple' to 'pair' with regard to people and 'couple' to 'few' with regard to minutes.
(b) Help children to listen to the endings on 'touched' and 'younger'.
(c) Listen to 'barber'. Discuss two families 'ar' and 'er' and add to both lists.
(d) Draw attention to 'le' ending. Most common way of making that sound at the end of English words.
(e) Discuss countries with a globe, or large map of the world.

a (ŏ)

sw**a**n	sw**a**llow
w**a**nt	sw**a**llowed
w**a**s	sw**a**p
w**a**sh	squ**a**sh
w**a**sp	squ**a**bble
wh**a**t	

Dictate the Sam and the Tramp Story

Gus and the policeman sat down and began to swallow sausages and beans. A bottle of squash was on the table with a glass.

"What would you like to drink? Do you want squash, or hot milk?"

"Squash, please," said Gus.

As the policeman gave him the glass, a wasp fell into the squash. The tramp did not see it and took a big gulp.

"Stop," said the policeman. "You've swallowed a wasp."

Pupils draw a line under the words in the 'a' family that look and sound like 'swan'.

New word: would

Words to practise: could, should

Read the Grandad Bill Story

As Holly and Harry began to squabble about the bits of the red boots, Grandad Bill said, "I could swallow a nice cup of tea, and so could Sam."

"Put the kettle on then," said his wife, "and get out the cups and saucers."

As they all sat down to drink tea, Grandad Bill said to Holly West, "I want to take you back to the shop to get green boots."

Holly gave a big swallow and said in a small voice, "Thank you, Grandad. My feet were so squashed in those red boots. I really do want green boots that fit."

"I should think so too," said Harry.

"Now you two," said Sad Gran. "Don't squabble."

Pupils identify and write 4 words with 'a' (ŏ) in them.

Teaching Points

(a) Link 'what' with 'wh question family' – who, what, why, when, which.
(b) Point our 'll' in swallowed and 'bb' in squabble.
(c) Remind of 'le' ending and link with squabble, bottle and table.
(d) Remind of abbreviation 'we've' (we have).

ph

phone
tele**ph**one
photo
ele**ph**ant

Philip
Philippa
micro**ph**one

Dictate the Sam and the Tramp Story

Gus felt the wasp and the squash disappear down his throat. One policeman rushed to the telephone to phone the hospital.

"This is the police station. P.C. Philip Brown speaking. One of our friends has swallowed a wasp. Can we bring him in to you?"

When the tramp heard the policeman on the phone call him their friend he began to feel very proud. P.C. Philip Brown left the telephone and came to the tramp with a microphone in his hand. "Open your mouth wide," he said. "Let's hear if the wasp is still buzzing."

Pupils draw a line under the words in the 'ph' family.

New words: heard, friend

Read the Grandad Bill Story

"I think we should phone your mother," said Grandad Bill and got his mobile phone.

"Look at this photograph," said Sad Gran to the twins. "This was taken when you were both tiny."

"Look, here's another photograph of an elephant at the Zoo."

"Can we go to the Zoo?" asked Holly.

"Not today," said Grandad Bill. "Come on. Get in the van. I've told your mother on the phone that we're going to get you some green boots that fit."

They gave the photographs back to Sad Gran and went out to the van. Sam picked up his tools and went home on his bent blue bike.

Pupils identify and write 3 words with 'ph' in them.

Teaching Points
(a) Discuss other things that begin with tele – television.
(b) Discuss uses of microphones and display one – or a picture.
(c) Link dis/ap/pear with 'ear' family and add to list.
(d) Link throat with 'oa' family and add to list.
(e) Break down hos/pit/al. Draw attention to 'al' ending.
(f) Remind of capital letters for names.

o (ō)

b **o** t h
p **o** s t
p **o** s t m a n
n **o**
s **o**
m **o** s t
o n l y

s **o** l d
t **o** l d
o l d
g **o** l d

Dictate the Sam and the Tramp Story

P.C. Brown put the old microphone into Gus's mouth. He told the others to be quiet so that he could hear. At first both the tramp and the policeman heard a faint buzzing. Then it stopped and the only sounds were the tramp's breathing and swallowing. P.C. Brown went back to the telephone and told the hospital that no buzzing could be heard.

"I think the wasp drowned in squash," he said.

Pupils draw a line under the words in the 'o' (ō) family that look and sound like 'both'.

New words: quiet, put

Word to practise: could

Read the Grandad Bill Story

Holly and Harry West both got into Sad Gran's van. They sat on the sand at the back. Grandad Bill told them to sit on the seat beside him, but they both liked sitting at the back.

"You can only sit there," Grandad told them, "if you find me some gold in that sand. I need it. Boots, stools and mending the bump in Sad Gran's van will take most of my cash."

The twins began to dig in the sand. If only they could find a little bit of gold to help Grandad. The van rushed along the High Street. It shot past the postman's van. "How much gold have you found?" asked Grandad.

"There's no gold in the sand," said Harry West.

"My hands, legs and dress are as yellow as gold," said Holly.

Pupils identify and write 4 words with 'o' (ō) in them.

Teaching Points

(a) Remind of apostrophe 's' – tramp's mouth.
(b) Link 'faint' with 'ai' family and add to list.
(c) Remind of doubling consonant to keep short vowel – stopped and buzzing.
(d) Speculate on what the tramp will do – after the dictation.
(e) Note the slight difference in pronounciation between 'both' and 'sold'.

are (air)

c **are**	sh **are**
sp **are**	sh **aring**
f **are**	h **are**
st **are**	d **are**
st **aring**	p **are** n t s

Dictate the Sam and the Tramp Story

Gus and P.C. Brown sat down again to share the spare sausages and beans. The tramp did not really care about the wasp inside him. He was happy to be sharing a meal with the policemen.

As they sat eating, Sam and his brother came into the police station.

Sam said, "I'm sorry to trouble you, but have you seen my friend the tramp?" The policemen stared at Gus, but he did not dare to look up.

Pupils draw a line under the words in the 'are' family that look and sound like 'care'.

New words: real, really

Word to practise: sorry

Read the Grandad Bill Story

As they got out of Sad Gran's van at the car park, Grandad Bill began staring at a man with a hood over his face and a sack in his hands. The man ran to the van. "Get back in, old man. Don't stand there staring." He jumped into the back and began to hide the sack in the sand. "Get in and drive off," he said.

"Don't you dare call Grandad an old man," said Harry West.

"We'll tell our parents about you," said Holly.

As the man turned to shake his fist at them Grandad jumped up behind him. He squashed the man's head down into the sand and sat on him. "Run like a hare, Harry and get the police," said Grandad. "Holly, rush to those gas men who are staring at us and tell them to come and help."

The man began to bump up and down in the sand but Grandad Bill held on. "I may be an old man," he said, "but I'm not frightened of you."

Pupils identify and write 3 words with 'are' (air) in them and 1 word ending with 'aring'.

Teaching Points
(a) Discuss 'fare' – bus fares etc.
(b) Point out rule – taking off 'e', to add 'ing'.
(c) Remind of 'trouble' family and of 'again'.
(d) Discuss why the tramp felt shy about looking at Sam.

ough

b **ough** t
th **ough** t
br **ough** t
ough t

Looks the same – sounds different

r **ough**
en **ough**
c **ough**
t **ough**

Dictate the Sam and the Tramp Story

"I thought I ought to ask about my friend," said Sam. "He looked rather rough with long hair and a beard."

The policemen began to laugh and P.C. Brown said to Sam, "You haven't looked hard enough."

Sam stared at the tramp in his new blue shirt and green trousers. Then Gus thought he ought to speak. He stood up. "This kind policeman brought me here," he said.

Sam slapped Gus hard on the back. He gave a cough and the wasp flew out of his mouth.

Pupils draw a line under the words in the 'ough' family. (They will not all sound the same.)

Read the Grandad Bill Story

Grandad Bill began to cough as he bumped up and down on the man's back. But he was tough enough not to let the man lift his head from the sand. Just then, Holly and three men came running across the car park. "Hold on Grandad," they shouted. "We're coming."

Then a police car drove into the car park with Harry sitting in the front. "I've brought the police, Grandad," he shouted. The police jumped out and dashed up to the van. "Take care, Grandad. He might get rough," they said.

They grabbed the man and his sack. Grandad got down from the van.

"Well done, Grandad," said Bob the policeman. "There is gold in the sack. This man has robbed the bank."

Pupils identify and write 4 words in the 'ough' family. (They will not all sound the same.)

Teaching Points
(a) Discuss the group of letters 'ough' and the three different sounds presented here.
(b) Put 'bought' and 'brought' into sentences when introducing them, to avoid the common confusion.
(c) Abbreviation – haven't (have not).
(d) Remind – 'pp' needed to keep short 'a' in slapped.

ar (or)

w **a** r	r e w **a r** d
w **a r** n	w **a r** d
w **a r** n i n g	q u **a r** t e r
w **a r** m	

Dictate the Sam and the Tramp Story

    At a quarter to two, Sue rushed into the police station. She had a warm coat over her nightdress. She was crying. "I want to offer a reward to anyone who can find my husband," she said as she sobbed. "I've phoned the hospital. My Sam is not in the wards there."

    Suddenly she saw Sam standing near her. She stopped crying and gave him a warm hug. "Come home," she said. "I will reward you with a nice slice of peach pie."

    Sue turned to the young man standing beside Sam in the blue shirt and green trousers. She saw his new brown boots, his smart beard and short hair.

    "Would you like to come home with us and share the peach pie and cream?" she asked him. She did not know it was the tramp and Sam did not explain. He thought she might change her mind if she found out and that would be dreadful.

    "We would both enjoy that," said Sam. "This is my old friend Augustus."

    "Thank you," said Augustus in a quiet voice. "I would love to come. Today is my birthday and I feel like a new man."

    "You are a new man," said Sam. "Happy birthday, Augustus. Have a glass of squash."

    "Happy birthday," sang all the others.

Pupils draw a line under the words in the 'ar' (or) family that look and sound like 'war'.

Read the Grandad Bill Story

    "Gold in the bag," said Grandad Bill. "Well, there was gold in my sand after all." He felt very warm now and was sweating.

    "But the gold won't help you, Grandad," said Harry.

    "Oh yes, there will be gold for Grandad," said Bob the policeman. "The bank is giving a reward. Grandad will get a quarter of this gold."

    "A quarter?" said Holly. "That will be a lot of money."

    Grandad looked happy and a warm smile spread across his face. "I'm so glad," he said. "But I never thought about a reward."

    "We're glad too," said the twins. "Good old Grandad."

Pupils identify and write 3 words in the 'ar' (or) family.

Teaching Points
(a) Teach only the new family.
(b) Give the pupils several opportunities to revise word families, in pairs and small groups.